WRITING, BLOGGING AND SELF-PUBLISHING

The Secret Formula For Writing Your First Book

KRIS BALLARD

WRITING, BLOGGING AND SELF-PUBLISHING

ISBN: 978-1-7333425-0-6

TABLE OF CONTENTS

DEDICATION

This book is dedicated to Marcie Morgan because she has inspired my writing.

ABOUT THE AUTHOR

Writing, Blogging and Self-Publishing, Kris Ballard's debut book, is the first of many books. Whenever he's not composing books, Ballard writes articles for his website: WebDevelopmentBlogger.com. Kris Ballard further enjoys helping people learn difficult concepts and topics. Kris Ballard is available for speaking engagements.

INTRODUCTION

This book is divided into three sections: writing, blogging, and self-publishing. While this is a lot of information to cover in a short book, I believe the information is beneficial to anyone wanting to learn these topics.

SECTION I: WRITING

CHAPTER 1: NONFICTION

Non-fiction writing involves you writing that which is true, or at least in theory it is. Sometimes, though, non-fiction is so fantastical that it is more unbelievable than fiction. This book is non-fiction.

While writing non-fiction, you will usually write an article or book. A lengthy blog post, in my view, would be considered an article.

If a novice writer is deciding whether or not to write a non-fiction book, they become overwhelmed. They don't know how they could write a short book. The good news is that it isn't as difficult as you might think.

Think of non-fiction writing as a collection of articles. Indeed, that is exactly what some non-fiction books are. I have read books that are collections of articles, written by the author who has previously published the articles elsewhere. Therefore, you will have enough content for a short book if you can write at least 10 - 11 articles that are at least 2,000 words.

Although, maybe you are not in a hurry to write a non-fiction book. In that case, you should focus more on writing articles. Many articles I have written have been published on my WordPress website. Another good place to publish articles is on Medium.

I used to write short articles when I began blogging; but now, I'm starting to write longer articles. I think a good length for an article is 2,000 words; though, it's up to you how many words you want to write.

One thing I have learned is that it's easy to get discouraged by comparing yourself to other writers. For example, I will be reading an article or book where writer says they usually write 1,000 words or more per hour. They thereby will recommend that everyone else should write this quickly as well.

While I'm sure these writers are only trying to be helpful, you wouldn't be reading this book if I took their advice seriously. The takeaway is that you should listen to advice but not always follow it. This is true even for the advice that I give you.

I would recommend reading the blogging section of this book if you want to learn about writing non-fiction articles. Now, let's return to our discussion about writing non-fiction.

It is very likely that you will need to do some research as you are writing your book. It is possible to write a book without any research; although, most non-fiction and fiction books will benefit from it.

There are two research mistakes which are made by many beginning writers. The first is that they don't complete enough research. I don't really understand this approach to writing. I have generally made the second mistake, which involves using too much research as a beginning writer.

Though taking the time to research your topic is a sensible idea, anything that is good can be overdone. I spent day after day researching a topic, while I wrote down a minimal amount of usable words. Don't be like I was. If you spend an hour researching a topic, but you only have thirty words written down, then you are spending too much time on research.

Next, we should discuss spelling. Misspelling words should be a rare occurrence with spell checkers available. Unfortunately, this is not the case. As much as I hate to brag, I was very good at spelling when I was in grade school. Nevertheless, some people struggle with it.

If you need to work on your spelling, this will be discussed in chapter five. Just remember, though, that being a good speller will make your life a lot easier.

As a beginning writer, you are probably wondering how much you should know before writing your book's first chapter. I knew what the title of the book would be as I began writing this book. Also, I knew how many chapters there would be, and what the chapters would be about.

Yet, I didn't know every single word that would be in the book. It is not necessary to know every detail before you write it. You will get bogged down in endless research if you insist on knowing all the details prior to writing.

While writing your first chapter, use the internet and other resources. This will ensure that you are actually getting words written down. Certain non-fiction genres will require a bit more research than would usually be necessary.

For instance, sometimes when I'm writing an article for my website and it's a complex topic, this takes longer to research. Still, I don't use that as an excuse for not being productive. In spite of the additional research, my articles are still completed within a reasonable amount of time.

It is a good idea to first read non-fiction if you are going to write it. I suggest signing up for Kindle Unlimited. Your first month will be free, and after that, it is only ten dollars a month. Kindle Unlimited gives you access to a million different eBooks. It is the best deal out there, so you should sign up immediately. You can thank me later for this advice.

Let's start talking about writing fiction now that we have finished discussing non-fiction writing. We will learn about this in the next chapter. I promise that you will enjoy it.

CHAPTER 2: FICTION

Fiction is when you write things that aren't based on facts. So why would anyone want to write something that isn't true? Well, when you look at all the published novellas and novels, you quickly realize a lot of people want to write about things that aren't true.

Not only are there a lot of people who want to write fiction, but there are also quite a few people who want to read it. While I haven't yet written a novella, I plan on writing one very soon. Whenever reading and writing fiction, however, be aware that there are different genres.

Two genres which I particularly like are science fiction and fantasy. There are also other popular genres such as romance, western, inspirational, and horror. As a beginning writer, you might be wondering whether or not you will be able to write an interesting novel.

My guess is that your novel will be much better than substandard novels which have been published over the years. Please be aware, though, that it is highly unlikely you will ever make as much money as J. K. Rowling through your writing.

Writing novels isn't a highly specialized skill of which only certain people are capable. Don't overthink writing your novel. Just tell your story, and possibly add a few insights along the way.

Good writing is good writing, regardless of which genre you choose when writing your novel. As you write, make sure that you write in your own distinctive style. It is alright to admire other novelists, but you need to share your own uniqueness with the world.

Also, don't plagiarize other people's writing. Don't pretend something is your idea when it isn't. This doesn't mean that you can't learn from other writers. It just means that you can't use entire sentences and paragraphs that other writers have already written.

This might seem like common sense, but unfortunately not everybody has common sense. So, save yourself a lot of trouble. Don't pretend to write something that somebody else has already written.

Once you have decided to write a novel, you need to figure out in which genre you will write. The first novella I write will be a historical novella set in the nineteenth century. In my novella, there will be a ship that sinks and some of the passengers will die.

You are already interested in reading this book, aren't you? Your novel can be just as exciting as the book that I intend to write.

However, you don't have to write a historical novel. You might want to write a book in the heroic fantasy genre. A good example of heroic fantasy would be: *The Hobbit.*

Another genre many people like to read and write is romance. It's not my cup of tea, but it might be something in which you are interested.

Then again, maybe you will want to explore the future with a science fiction novel. Some of the best books that I have read were written in this genre. The best science fiction book I have read is *The World Inside,* written by Robert Silverberg.

It's time to start writing after you have decided which genre that you want to use for your novel. You can do some research along the way, but don't overdo it. Sometimes endless research can prevent you from actually getting anything written down.

Also, remember that not every sentence that you write is going to be brilliant. If you can write a story worth reading, and that has some literary merit, then you are doing better than most writers.

You are wrong if you think enough novels have already been written. I will agree, however, that too many bad novels have been written. So, just make sure that you are writing a book of which you can be proud.

For instance, if you are writing a science fiction novel, don't just write about spaceships and laser guns. Use the example of Robert Silverberg. Write about an overpopulated world that is actually quite awful.

Don't write an average book if you are writing a historical novel. Instead, write a book like Victor Hugo wrote when he composed *The Hunchback of Notre-Dame.* If your historical novel is half as good as Victor Hugo's, than you will have produced a masterpiece.

Some people think that judging the quality of fiction is entirely subjective. However, I believe that it is possible to fairly critique novels and novellas. Even if I was to read a book in a genre that I usually don't like, I am confident I could properly evaluate that novel or novella.

This doesn't mean that all book critics are always going to agree with each other. There is obviously room for disagreement when critics are reviewing novels. Also, most novels that are written are neither great nor terrible.

Instead of saying that this particular novel is lousy, it would probably be better to say that this novel is a 55 on a scale of one to 100. Likewise, if you are reading a very good novel, it would be more informative to say that this book is an 84.

I have included this chapter on fiction in this book because I don't want writers to think they are only capable of writing non-fiction. It is good to expand your horizons and also write fiction.

The next chapter in this book is about research. This chapter will help you whether you are writing fiction or nonfiction. Even though I have cautioned you about doing too much research, that doesn't mean that you shouldn't do any research at all.

CHAPTER 3: RESEARCH

Writing requires some research. It is possible to write a book without research, so you will should at least research how to spell certain words. The best research advice that I can give you is to sign up with Amazon Unlimited.

Amazon Unlimited will give you access to a million eBooks for only ten dollars a month. The first month is free, and if you don't like it, you can discontinue your service without paying anything. Amazon Unlimited is the best deal that I have seen, and I am not a young person.

It's an awesome feeling when you have access to a million eBooks. Some eBooks aren't covered with Amazon Unlimited, but you have the option of purchasing them if you feel they are worth the expense.

Another resource that I would suggest for research is Grammar Girl. Mignon Fogarty, who started Grammar Girl, is a genius. You can learn a lot about grammar from her podcast. Chapter six discusses this resource in greater depth.

The next resource that I will suggest for research is Udemy. Udemy is a website that offers online courses. Some of the courses are free, but some cost money. There are always special prices for the courses; at the same time, if you are willing to wait several days, you can enroll in a course for ten dollars.

Udemy courses range from forty minutes to forty hours. I usually sign up for courses in the three- to ten-hour range. While learning from Udemy instructors is beneficial, is assures you aren't plagiarizing the video lectures.

The video lectures on Udemy are a great way to get ideas for the book that you are writing. Also, there are lectures on Udemy which can help you with your grammar. I originally started watching videos on Udemy because I wanted to learn JavaScript.

Nevertheless, even though I still haven't mastered JavaScript, I have learned a lot of other valuable things from Udemy. If you sign up for a three-hour lecture on Udemy, it will probably take longer than three hours to watch the video.

This is because there is so much information in a video. You will sometimes need to pause the video in order to take notes. Sometimes the instructors will ask you to take quizzes, or access additional resources on the internet.

Some of the instructors on Udemy have accents. So, make sure you understand what the teacher is saying before you sign up for his or her course. That being said, I still think that Udemy is a fantastic research resource for writers.

The next research resource is so obvious; you will probably wonder why I'm even mentioning it. Maybe you haven't really bothered to use Wikipedia all that much. If you haven't, than you are making a big mistake. Even though your research should involve more than Wikipedia, this online encyclopedia is a good place to start. I find Wikipedia to be especially useful when I'm writing articles for my website.

I further found Wikipedia to be helpful when I was writing about fiction in previous chapter. So, go ahead and use Wikipedia as a research tool.

I hate to sound like an old man, but the younger generation doesn't realize what awesome research tools they have at their fingertips. I was born in the last year (1964) of the baby boom. The World Wide Web wasn't even invented until I had been an adult.

So, if you are a younger writer, be grateful for the research resources that are available to you. Let me share a great research resource that I don't use nearly enough. This resource is called Khan Academy.

I feel so much smarter every time I access Khan Academy. The video lectures about World War I at Khan Academy are brilliant. There are many subjects which you can study at Khan Academy. Salman Khan is the person who started this educational resource. The courses at Khan Academy are free, and anyone can benefit from them.

You score points as you watch video lectures, or when you do well on quizzes. It may sound silly, but it is fun to rack up a bunch of points.

At Khan Academy, you are also awarded badges for your progress. I definitely recommend using Khan Academy as a research tool.

Now, I'm going to suggest using a research resource more obvious than Wikipedia: YouTube. When you are on YouTube, you don't have to spend all of your time watching funny cat videos.

Believe it or not, you can actually educate yourself. I have learned a lot about web development and web design, simply by watching YouTube videos. You also have the ability to comment on the YouTube videos you watch.

I have even spoken to a university professor who recommends using YouTube as an educational resource. The main takeaway here is that you should use YouTube as a research resource for your writing.

The last research resource that I'm going to mention is the public library. You can tap into the Wi-Fi at the library while using it on your laptop. Also, there are all those wonderful books at the library which are waiting to be checked out.

If you are doing research about computers or technology, some of the books will be too old. This is because computer technology, and technology in general, is changing so rapidly. However, you can get around this limitation by using some of the other research resources previously mentioned.

The public library is your friend while writing your book or an article for your website. This concludes this chapter on research, and now it's time for the chapter about sentences.

CHAPTER 4: SENTENCES

You have to write a lot of sentences if you write a book. You don't have to be Shakespeare, but you do have to get your ideas across. While writing your book, you will need to write a specific amount number of words each day.

For example, this book is about 21,000 words. So, I quickly realized I would have to write 210 words a day. That is if I wanted to finish writing this book in a timely manner.

It may sound odd I'm writing about sentences when I struggle with grammar myself. However, this might be one of those situations where it is so wrong that it's right.

The first thing to be aware of whenever writing sentences is to avoid writing sentence fragments. How do you know if you are accidentally writing a sentence fragment?

You will know because your sentence doesn't contain a complete thought. There is more to it than that, but this is a good starting point.

A true sentence isn't going to confuse the reader. Your reader doesn't have to agree with every sentence, but your sentences should make sense. Sometimes a fragment can be combined with another sentence. If you do this correctly, you can convert your fragment into a true sentence.

Believe it or not, though, there are instances when you should use sentence fragments. For example, it's alright to use fragments if you are creating a bulleted list.

Using fragments is also alright if you're an advertiser. The main takeaway about sentence fragments is that you need to know the rules before you break them.

Now let's talk about run-on sentences. A run-on sentence is a sentence that tries to do too much. While this may sound complicated, run-on sentences can be corrected with punctuation.

You might think all run-on sentences are long sentences. On the contrary, a run-on sentence can be a short sentence. You book will be full of comma splices and fused sentences, should you not punctuate your sentences correctly.

Is the world going to collapse if you make a few mistakes with your grammar? Probably not, but do your readers a favor. Write the best sentences you possibly can.

Maybe it's wrong, but I worried less about grammar whenever writing articles for my website, instead of when I was writing this book. I will be able to use what I have learned through writing this book, though, in order to create better articles in the future.

Your writing will dramatically improve with the more you write. You might say that writing is like swimming. The only way you will become a good writer is by jumping into the water.

This might be a little frightening at first, but eventually you will gain confidence in your ability to write. My hope is that this book helps you in becoming an outstanding writer. Now, let's get back to learning how to create sentences.

Transitional words and phrases are needed to create good sentences; without these, your writing won't seem quite right. Transitions, too, improve your paragraphs.

It takes a while, but eventually you will get the hang of using transitions. Using transitional words and phrases will make your writing smoother and more understandable. By adding words in the right places, you will improve your writing.

While studying grammar, you will be surprised with how many strange words and concepts there are. But then, you quickly realize that grammar is your friend after learning different terminology.

Grammar experts say sentences can be improved by using the active voice. Many beginning writers, though, fall into the trap of using the passive voice. I recently discovered that I was primarily writing in the passive voice.

I became aware of this through blogging. I primarily write my articles on WordPress where I eventually installed a plug-in that told me I was using the passive voice.

At first, I was humiliated, but I soon owned up to it. Now my writing is better than it was. I'm still learning how to properly use the active voice myself. So, I will do the best that I can to point you in the right direction.

You have to understand subjects and verbs when you are writing in the active voice. The type of subject about which I'm talking isn't the subject of your book. Instead, this is the subject of your sentence.

For instance: Gandalf, Green Lantern, Batman, and Doctor Strange, are fictional examples of subjects in a sentence. Obviously, there are also non-fiction subjects in sentences.

The next part of using the active voice is realizing how the subject of a sentence interacts with the verb. For example: *The Hunchback of Notre-Dame rang the bell.* This is how you should use the active voice. Don't write: *The bell was rung by the Hunchback of Notre-Dame.* Can you see the difference?

When you seriously thinking about sentences and grammar, you realize that you have a lot to learn; however, don't let that discourage you. Just think of it as an adventure.

CHAPTER 5: SPELLING

Years ago as a small child, I wasn't very good at spelling. Then my teacher told me that, since I was good at reading, she couldn't figure out why I was having trouble with my spelling.

So, when I thought about it, I couldn't figure out why I was having trouble with my spelling either. Well, I started paying attention in class to what the teacher was telling about spelling. Soon after, I became a great speller.

If you are reading this book, I'm guessing that you are already good at spelling. So, why write an entire chapter about spelling? I want you to become a great speller.

Even if you never write a book, you don't want to embarrass yourself by making spelling mistakes. You can always improve your spelling, regardless of what level it's at currently. So, let's get started with working on our spelling.

The first thing to understand about the English language is that when it comes to spelling, this language doesn't always make sense. Over the years, I have heard many people say how the spelling of certain words should be changed.

Well, until the day arrives when all these spelling changes are made, we are stuck with what we already have. Also, you are wrong if you think that the spell checker on your computer is going to correct all of your spelling mistakes.

I know that I'm being blunt, but my goal is to help you with your spelling. If I was to go along with every excuse that people make for not being great spellers, than there would be no purpose for me to write this chapter.

We will be covering is American English in this chapter. The British spell many of their words differently, so if you want to learn the British spellings, that can be your research assignment.

It is good to learn some of the spelling rules when you are trying to improve your spelling. I will admit that I have forgotten many of the spelling rules which I learned while in grade school. However, it is my intention to relearn some of them.

One spelling rule I do remember is that i comes before e, except after c. There are exceptions to this rule, such as: ancient, beige, caffeine, deist, and Einstein. This may sound like a very simple rule, but surprisingly, there are many people who don't follow it.

Let's try out another spelling rule. In the English language, nearly every q is followed by the letter u. Thinking about this rule, it really is difficult to find words that break it. Some exceptions to this rule are: burqa, Iraqi, qi, qwerty, and umiaq. If you don't know what umiaq is, it's a type of boat. Qi is another way to spell chi. As you can see, there are a lot of interesting words about which to learn.

Are you ready for another spelling rule? The letter s never follows the letter x. For example, the plural of box is boxes. To put the s directly next to the x wouldn't look right. I have not found any exceptions to this rule.

The next spelling rule is this: English words don't end in the letter i. This rule is generally true; however, there are exceptions to this rule: fungi, Wi-Fi and bikini.

Can you see how simple spelling rules can help with spelling? There are a lot of other spelling rules, but this should get you started.

Sometimes it's good to look at commonly misspelled words when you are working on your spelling. Some of the words on these types of lists might be easy for you to spell. Although, some of the words could be more challenging.

Here is a short list of commonly misspelled words I have compiled for you: accumulate, analyze, bizarre, business, colonel, committee, dilemma, embarrass, envelope, Fahrenheit, foreign, government, innuendo, necessary, pneumonia, siege, and weird.

If you want to learn more about commonly misspelled words, than type the phrase "commonly misspelled words" into a search engine. Many grammar books also have these types of lists.

Are you ready for something that you probably haven't thought much about since grade school? Let's take a look at homophones. Homophones are words that are pronounced the same, but they don't mean the same thing.

For instance: to, too, and two. I know that this is very basic; though, but I see mistakes with simple words like these in text messages and emails that I receive.

Let's try something more difficult: then and than. These two words sound the same, but they have different meanings. Spelling these two words correctly might be easy for you, but I'm embarrassed to admit I often get these words mixed up.

Use the word then whenever something relates to time. Use than when you are making a comparison. Now, I just need to remember my own advice.

The next homophone with which we will experiment is weather and whether. When I was a child, I understood the difference between these two words. The problem, though, was remembering that there is a letter h in whether.

Let's conclude our study of homophones with one more example. How about ware, wear, and where? In order to spell these words correctly, we need to know what each word means.

Ware mean merchandise or pottery. Wear is the clothing in which you dress, and where is a physical place. You might ask: "Where were you?"

We have learned a lot about spelling in this chapter. Hopefully this information will help you improve your writing skills.

CHAPTER 6: GRAMMAR GIRL®

Grammar Girl is an online resource that I mentioned in *Research* (chapter three). Mignon Fogarty began Grammar Girl, and I'm very glad that she did. When you use this website, you will have the option of reading the articles, or you can have the articles read to you on the podcast.

I prefer to listen to the podcasts on Stitcher. To get started, find Grammar Girl at: quickanddirtytips.com/grammar-girl. I just finished listening to episode #670, titled: *Equinox. Is Irish the Same as Gaelic?*

Grammar Girl will learn a little bit about everything. Mignon Fogarty might not increase the quantity of your writing, but she can help improve the quality of your writing.

Another great Grammar Girl episode to which I have listened is episode #680: *Wakanandan, Groot, and Other Languages.* Through this podcast, you will learn about the different languages that are spoken by different characters in the Marvel movies. Furthermore, you will learn about Easter. It might seem random to combine these topics into a single podcast until you realize that this podcast was created in April.

If you are not familiar with podcasting, a podcast is an awesome way to access audio content on your computer. You can find podcasts about any subject.

To be honest, though, there are a lot of people who create low quality podcasts of which aren't worth listening. That's alright, though, because I have trouble keeping up with the podcasts that I do like. I can say with complete confidence the Grammar Girl podcast is worthy of your time.

Now, let's explore episode #655: *'Myriad' or 'Myriad Of'*? What is a run-on sentence? I especially admire this episode, because it talks a lot about how to create great sentences. *Sentences* (chapter four) was also about sentences.

In this particular episode, Mignon Fogarty really emphasizes run-on sentences aren't necessarily long sentences. This episode will teach you about the importance of correctly punctuating your sentences.

Grammar Girl has so many great episodes, making it is difficult to decide which one is the best. My favorite episode is #674: *How You Can Benefit Year-Round from NanoWriMo.*

NanoWriMo is an organization which encourages ordinary people to write a 50,000-word novel during the month of November. Although I have no desire to write 50,000 words in a month, I am impressed with the idea of helping others learn how to write.

You have to write if you want to be a writer. Having great ideas won't help you if you aren't able to get a little bit written down each day. It's not a lack of time which will prevent you from writing. I work a full-time job, but I still found the time to write this book.

Also, don't use being a slow typist as an excuse for not writing. No matter how slowly you type, I promise you that I'm slower. So if I can get words written down, than you certainly can.

Now that we are done with the pep talk, let's look at another Grammar Girl podcast episode to which you should listen. This is episode #610: *Top 10 Grammar Myths.*

This is a great podcast, because it shows some ideas about grammar are wrong. Though, don't feel bad; I'm also still learning new things about grammar.

The next segment of episode #610 is about dog breeds. If you love dogs, than you should listen to this segment. Grammar Girl explains the name origins of thirteen different types of dogs.

Another good Grammar Girl podcast episode is #587, titled: *More British and American Differences.* If you had any doubts American English and British English are different, you certainly won't after listening to this episode.

Mignon Fogarty starts the podcast by giving a lengthy explanation of why British writers think of companies in the plural. This is different than in America where we think of companies in the singular.

If this sounds confusing, than listen to this episode, Therefore, you can understand this concept. I will say, though, that the British way of doing things can lead to sentences which sound nonsensical to most Americans.

In episode #587, Mignon Fogarty also has a segment where she explains how the British use quotation marks. British use these differently than Americans do. If you think that grammar is a dry subject, than you may change your opinion after listening to an episode of Grammar Girl.

I know that it's sad, but we only have time to review a few more episodes of Grammar Girl in this chapter. Episode #676 is about the Game of Thrones television show. Mignon Fogarty didn't write this episode, but she reads the podcast.

Since I have never watched Game of Thrones, this episode did a good job of explaining what the program is about. The reason that Grammar Girl is interested in the Game of Thrones is because there are eleven languages in this TV show.

Obviously, the languages spoken on Game of Thrones aren't real languages. These are languages that were created by a fellow with way too much time on his hands. Even if you are not planning on watching the Game of Thrones, this is a good episode in which to listen.

The final Grammar Girl episode I will review is #639. In this episode, Mignon Fogarty gives some common sense tips about how to construct a great paragraph.

Spoiler alert: there is a lot more to writing a great paragraph than you think. Now it is time to learn about LibreOffice Writer.

CHAPTER 7: LIBREOFFICE WRITER

Upon beginning to write a book, you will need to decide which word processing software you want to use. LibreOffice Writer is what I'm using while typing this book. Obviously, you can choose any word processing software with which you feel comfortable.

While there are many types of word processing software, I only have experience with three of them. These are LibreOffice Writer, Google Docs, and Microsoft Word.

I would still recommend reading this chapter even if you decide not to use LibreOffice Writer. This information will also help you better understand your word processing software.

First, LibreOffice Writer is free. You can donate money for it if you want, but you don't have to do this. The organization which controls LibreOffice Writer is called The Document Foundation.

As you download LibreOffice Writer, you are also downloading the entire LibreOffice suite. LibreOffice is similar to Microsoft Office, or the suite offered by Google.

In this chapter, we will be focusing on the LibreOffice Writer section of the LibreOffice suite. If you are familiar with Microsoft Word, than LibreOffice Writer will be easy for you to learn.

When you are using LibreOffice Writer, there are a lot of different fonts from which to choose. The default font is called Liberation Serif.

With Writer, you can choose the font size you prefer. I use the 18-font size for my paragraphs, and the 22-font size for my chapter headings. If you need to align or justify your paragraph, than Writer can do that too.

LibreOffice Writer is able to change the background color, as well as the font color of your document. It is very unlikely that you will need to use every feature that Writer offers. However, it's nice to know that these features are available.

The bulleted list and numbered list can come in handy with many types of writing. Just remember that there are little arrows on which you can click. These will increase the options you have for creating lists.

When you make a mistake with your writing, Writer has an undo button which is located at the top of your page. While at the top of your page, you will also notice that there are cut, copy, and paste buttons.

Whenever you are typing your book, Writer will automatically save what you are writing. This is good, because who wants to lose their hard work? You can also click on the save button if you want to save your writing more frequently.

As you start writing your book, you will need to hit the save as button. This allows you to create a title for you document. Otherwise, your document will be labeled as being untitled.

It's also important to know how to select your text. I was originally going to suggest highlighting your text, but then I discovered that wasn't what I was trying to say. Text highlighting is when you use different colors to highlight portions of your text.

Nevertheless, selecting text is much more basic. If you want to select a word, double-click that word. Triple-click a word in the sentence if you need to select a sentence. You are further able to select an entire paragraph by quadruple-clicking a word in that paragraph.

LibreOffice Writer also has spell checking. Although Writer has a good spell checker, you still need to review *Spelling* (chapter five) of this book. If you think that you don't need to know how to spell because Writer has a spellchecker, than you are wrong.

Spell checking is a nice feature, but don't let it lull you into a false sense of security. Fortunately, if you have trouble spelling, you can improve in this area. Although I'm already good at spelling, I plan on becoming an even better speller.

To become knowledgeable about Writer, I would suggest downloading the Writer guide. You can find this guide in LibreOffice Writer's help section. It's a comprehensive guide, and I'm still reading it myself.

Another top-notch resource for explaining Writer is Udemy. Vicki Watson has an amazing video course on Udemy, which describes all the features that Writer has to offer. If you wait for a special, you can watch this six-hour course for only ten dollars.

Conversely, you should finish reading this chapter first before you get started with these two resources. There are several more things that I would like to share with you.

As you start writing a book, you have a general idea of how many words will be within your book. Therefore, you can calculate how many words you should write each day.

This is where LibreOffice Writer comes in handy. Just look at the bottom of your document, and you will see how many words you have written. Before I start writing each day, I look at my total word count. I don't stop writing until I have written at least 210 words.

This might not sound like much, but even 210 words a day adds up. I also do a little writing on my website each day, but I don't use Writer for these articles. I will share my blogging methods with you in the blogging section of this book.

The last tip about Writer which I will share is that Writer allows you to add images to your documents. I'm still learning how to use this feature, but it's nice to know that it's there if I need it.

We have just completed the writing section of this book. So, now it's time to move on to the blogging section. Here you will learn how to write and publish online articles.

SECTION II: BLOGGING

CHAPTER 8: DECIDING ON A NICHE

There are a lot of people who have dabbled with blogging, but not many people have truly mastered it. Although, I feel that I have learned quite a lot about blogging. I'm still learning new ways to improve my blog.

For those unaware, blogging is when you write and publish articles on the internet. At least, that's my definition of blogging. There is a lot more to blogging than that, but let's use this definition as a starting point.

Articles which you write can be fifty words or five-thousand words. It's up to you how much you write. It's also up to you how often you write. If you are writing five-thousand-word articles, though, you are probably not going to post your articles as often as someone writing fifty-word articles.

When you start blogging, your natural instinct will be to blog about anything and everything. That's what I did. Although you may think this is the right way to blog, you actually are wrong.

When you're blogging, you have to decide on a niche. For instance, my website is titled: Web Development Blogger. The subtitle for my website is: Web Development, Blogging, and Podcasting.

This doesn't mean that I can't ever go slightly off-topic while I'm blogging, but it does mean I need to focus on my niche. If you think that this approach to blogging will stifle your creativity, than let me share my solution to this problem.

The website Medium is where I plan on publishing my off-topic articles. I'm currently writing an article about Extra Dimensions which I plan on publishing on Medium. I wouldn't publish this article on my own website because it is too far off-topic. It would merely confuse my readers if I was to publish this article on my WordPress website.

I will talk more about the Medium website, in *Medium* (chapter eleven) of this book. For now, Medium is a website about which you should learn more.

It may take you some time to decide on your niche. Some beginning bloggers make the mistake of creating several different websites. If you do this, your attention will be so scattered that none of your blogs will be any good.

If you planning on writing a book, than the advice that I'm giving you is especially relevant. When you start writing a book, the time for blogging will be limited.

So, the main takeaway here is that blogging on multiple websites while having a niche isn't a good strategy. The rest of this chapter will primarily be about helping you decide on the best niche for your blog.

The first step to choosing a niche for your website is to pick something about which you enjoy writing. If you are not interested in what you are writing about it, then it is unlikely you will get many words written down.

Being interested in something doesn't mean that every moment of your blogging career will be sheer bliss. Writing is hard work. Don't let anyone tell you that it isn't. That being said, writing should never be something that you dread.

Whether I'm working on this book, or writing an article for my blog, I am always pleased whenever I get some words written down. As I have already said in *Grammar Girl* (chapter six): you have to write if you want to be a writer.

Now, let's look at some ideas on how to decide if a niche is ideal for your blog. One idea is to start a lifestyle blog. The blog: Just a girl and her blog. This is the best example which I have seen.

This blog was created by Abby Lawson. She has a lot of great things to say about organizing, decorating, and blogging. Abby's husband helps her with the blog, and their blog is very popular.

The reason that this blog is successful? Abby didn't try to be all things to all people. Instead, she found a niche and she stuck with it.

The topics that you can choose for your blog's niche are limitless. Let's look at a few more possibilities in order to give you a better idea of how to decide on a niche for your blog.

Maybe you want to teach other people how to save money. Well, you are in luck; there is a frugal living category of blogs. No, I'm not making this up. Believe it or not, you can make money by teaching other people how to save money.

There are a lot of different strategies for saving money. You can be a great help to other people if you are willing to share your expertise. If you are blogging about frugal living, than I would suggest writing a book on this topic as well.

Another popular niche to consider is travel. I like to read travel blogs; although, I don't know if I would ever write one. You might be someone who wants to create a travel blog. The first step to becoming a travel blogger is being someone who travels on a regular basis. Therefore, you have something about which to blog. It will be difficult to instruct other people on how to travel if you are a homebody.

Now that we have thought a little bit about blogging niches, it is up to you to decide what your blog should be about. You will need to do some research. Then, start blogging. Now, let's learn about content marketing.

CHAPTER 9: CONTENT MARKETING

The first time that I heard of content marketing, I had no idea what it was. Fortunately, I now know what it is. I will explain to you why content marketing is such a powerful concept.

When you create a website and write articles for it, you are creating content. When you start blogging, you automatically become a content creator.

However, smart people quickly realized that merely creating content wasn't enough. They figured that, as long as you are going to the effort of creating content for your blog, you might as well market that content.

While content marketing is a simple concept, most people and companies aren't doing it the right way. You might be wondering if you should take the time to learn about content marketing.

The answer to this question yes – that is if you want your content to reach a larger audience than yourself. Then, you need to learn about content marketing. I promise that the time you spend learning about content marketing will be a wise use of your time.

Learning the finer points of content marketing is also fun. I have to admit that content marketing isn't the dull subject which I originally thought it was.

You will need to learn several basic ideas in order to get started with content marketing. First, content marketing is not just about blogging.

I know that I placed content marketing in the blogging section of this book. However, content marketing also deals with video, podcasting, eBooks, checklists, interviews, social media, etc. Content marketing is a topic that you really to study in a serious way.

If you are reading this book, then there is a good chance that you are interested in writing and self-publishing a book. So naturally, after you publish your book, you will want people to buy it.

This is where content marketing enters the picture. Let's say that you start out by publishing a paperback version of you book. Later on, you also decide to publish your book in eBook and audio book formats.

How should you market the three versions of your book? Well, let's pretend that you have already created your own podcast, and that people enjoy listening to it. If this is true, your loyal listeners will want you to tell them about your book.

Can you already see how content marketing is different from traditional advertising? With content marketing, you are sharing useful information with people who are already interested in what you have to say.

Let's look at another way to sell your book. While content marketing is awesome, you can also combine this method with email marketing. Email marketing may seem old-fashioned, but it is still effective.

It's never alright to spam people with email marketing. If you don't have permission to send someone an email, than don't.

At the same time, if you have been doing your content marketing correctly, your fans will be happy to receive your emails. Building an email list is a big part of email marketing. You need to get people to subscribe to your email list.

Since your email list will eventually become quite large, you will not want to put all of your subscribers on your personal email service. If you are blogging on WordPress, I would suggest using MailPoet for your email subscriber list.

Once you have your email list, let your subscribers know you have written a book. Ask them if they want to buy your masterpiece. Even if some of your fans don't want to buy your book, you have still done the right thing by sharing valuable information with them.

As you can see, email marketing is an important topic you need to study. It might not seem fair I'm asking you to learn so much. You will thank me later for my advice.

Social media marketing is another type of marketing which works well with content marketing. There are a lot of people who use Facebook, Twitter, and Pinterest.

Whether you like or hate social media, you need to reach people wherever they are located. So make sure you share articles you have written on several different social media websites.

Then, people can learn about your blog as they are reading your article on Twitter. Furthermore, they can read other articles that you have written. Sometimes people will want to interact with you on the various social media platforms, and that's alright too.

All of the articles that you write should have social media buttons on which your fans can click. The reason for this is because you want to make it easy for people to share your content.

If you do this correctly, content marketing and social media marketing can work beautifully together. Use social media to your advantage. Don't waste your time watching funny cat videos.

If you are going to spend time on social media, make sure that you are being productive. Instead of telling your friends on Facebook about your political opinions, tell them about the book that you have just written.

I have barely scratched the surface in describing content marketing. You will need to do additional research on this topic if you want to make a good income with writing or podcasting.

Content marketing doesn't just help you with selling your content. It can also help you with selling products and services. When you do content marketing in the right way, people will want to buy whatever you are selling.

I hope you are just as excited about content marketing as I am.

CHAPTER 10: WORDPRESS

I recommend using WordPress when you are ready to start your blog. You can build a website with WordPress, and your blog will be part of your website. If you want to be a serious blogger, than I suggest using the WordPress.org version of WordPress.

You will need to get a web-hosting service in order to use WordPress.org. I use is Bluehost, and it costs $2.95 per month.

There is always a chance you won't like blogging, but even if you decide you don't want to blog anymore, you can still use your website for podcasting or e-commerce.

Still, you will probably enjoy blogging if you give it the time and attention that it deserves.

When blogging, it is good to set goals for yourself. For example, I type at least 105 words on my personal WordPress blog each day. This is only half as much as I write on my book each day.

The only exception that I have to this rule is if I'm writing an article for the Medium platform. Then, the 105 words I normally would write for my WordPress website are instead written for my Medium article.

I talk more about Medium in the next chapter. When it comes to writing articles, my main focus is to blog on my personal website.

Sometimes it's easy to forget your WordPress website can be used for other things besides blogging. For instance, you can also use your personal website for podcasting.

I am still learning how to podcast, but I know it will add a new dimension to my WordPress website. As you learn more about WordPress, you will realize it is possible for you to build a website of which you can be proud.

In this chapter, though, we will primarily be discussing how to use WordPress for blogging. When you are blogging on WordPress, you will be working with the Gutenberg editor.

There has been some controversy surrounding Gutenberg. There are people who have used the classic editor for many years, and they don't want to upgrade to Gutenberg.

All the while, I love Gutenberg and I'm glad that WordPress has decided to use a new editor. When you use Gutenberg, you will quickly discover that it is based on blocks. The most common block you will use while typing your articles is the paragraph block.

Gutenberg also has blocks for heading, sub-headings, quotes, images, etc. It takes a while to get used to using blocks, but you will enjoy using Gutenberg after you do.

One of the first things about which you will learn when using WordPress is themes. The theme that you decide to use will control the appearance and functionality of your website.

Some WordPress themes are free, while other themes can cost fifty or sixty dollars. The theme that I use for my WordPress website is called Atomic Blocks. Atomic Blocks is a free theme, and it is compatible with the Gutenberg editor.

It may take you some time to find a theme you like, but that's alright. If you can't decide on which theme you want to use, just use a temporary theme for now.

Another thing you will must learn about WordPress is how to use plug-ins. You may think that plug-ins should have a hyphen, but strangely enough, WordPress doesn't use a hyphen when they are spelling plugins.

The reason you need to know about WordPress plug-ins is because they add functionality to your website. There are over fifty-thousand WordPress plug-ins available – all of which help you improve your website.

However, don't get carried away by installing too many plug-ins. By doing this, you could end up breaking your website. Less is more when it comes to WordPress plug-ins.

One plug-in I recommend everyone installing is Yoast SEO. It will help you with your search engine optimization.

Search Engine Optimization (SEO) is a technique that helps search engines find your content.

If you do SEO correctly, then you can get your articles ranked better on various search engines. However, by doing SEO the wrong way, you will only prove you are an obnoxious buffoon.

This is why it is important to use Yoast SEO on your website. If you don't want to use Yoast SEO, find a similar SEO plug-in with which you are comfortable.

When you are blogging on WordPress, you are using a very powerful content management system. I have heard there are other good content management systems, such as Joomla and Drupal.

My knowledge of those systems is minimal; so, if you want to learn these systems then you will have to teach yourself.

If you want to take your WordPress knowledge to the next level, I would recommend watching video courses on Udemy. Not only will you find courses there which will help you understand WordPress, but you will also find courses which will help in improving your blogging skills. Consider spending ten dollars on a Udemy course as an investment in yourself.

Kindle Unlimited is another good resource for improving your blogging skills. With Kindle Unlimited, you only have to pay ten dollars a month to get started. If you don't like

Kindle Unlimited, you can quit after the first month without paying anything.

The main takeaway from this chapter is that you need to start blogging as soon as possible. As you learn how to use WordPress, your confidence in your blogging skills will grow. Also, remember to use your best writing skills when you are blogging.

CHAPTER 11: MEDIUM

Medium is an online website that you can use for blogging. I recommend using Medium for writing off-topic articles. These articles don't fit into the niche that you have created for your WordPress website.

The nice thing about Medium is that they will pay you for your writing. The amount of money that you make depends on how popular your articles are.

Medium has a complex formula that determines the exact amount of money that you will make. It is unlikely you will make enough money on Medium on which to live, but something is better than nothing.

Be aware that, while blogging on Medium, they don't allow advertising. If you want to advertise, save it for your WordPress website. Personally, I'm glad that Medium doesn't allow advertising.

I haven't actually written an article for Medium; however, I am currently writing an article about extra dimensions that I plan to publish on Medium. This article will discuss research that is taking place in the fields of physics and mathematics.

Obviously, you will need to decide if Medium is a blogging platform where you wish to publish some of your articles.

Even if you never publish an article on Medium, I suggest reading many of the articles that have been published on their website.

Medium also allows you to follow the writers that you like. This feature is similar to following people on Twitter.

While I have known about Medium for a long time, it wasn't until recently that I realized exactly how much content has been published on this website. It's a bit like thinking that there are fifty books in the Library of Congress. Then, you realize there are more books in that library than you can imagine.

So, start off by exploring the content that is available on Medium. Later on, you will probably want to publish some of your articles on this blogging platform.

My blogging strategy is to publish one out of every three articles which I write on Medium. However, you will need to decide which blogging strategy works best for you.

When you start blogging on Medium, you will need to know more than someone who is only reading the articles. A good way to learn more about blogging on Medium is to watch video courses on Udemy.

A Udemy video course about Medium I would recommend watching is titled: *Medium Blogging Masterclass.* Sinem Gunel teaches this course. She shows you Medium strategies that would take a long time to learn on your own.

Sometimes, though, the audio in this video course isn't loud enough. So, be prepared to turn the volume up on your laptop. That being said, this course is still worth watching.

Part of being successful on Medium is becoming part of the Medium community. You can do this by making comments on articles that you read.

If you like an article on Medium, you can give it a clap. While learning more about Medium, you will realize there is a lot more to it than you originally thought.

Some of the terminology on Medium can be confusing for beginners. For instance, the word publications is used to refer to online magazines that are located on the Medium website.

It is important to get your articles published within these online magazines, thereby giving many people the opportunity to read what you write. You first have to get permission in order to publish your articles in these publications.

Another option is to start your own publication where writers will need to ask for your permission to publish their articles within your online magazine.

One thing that I have noticed about the Medium blogging platform is this: when I read articles there, I genuinely want to follow other writers. Not only do I want to follow these writers on Medium, but I also want to follow them on Twitter.

I have also noticed, too, that many writers on Medium get a lot of comments about their articles. This is great, because most writers enjoy have feedback on their writing.

Sometimes when you are writing, you begin to wonder if anyone is going to read what you have written. With Medium, you will be able to interact with your readers.

I still recommend publishing at least two-thirds of your content with Medium, while also publishing exclusively on your own WordPress website.

I believe that bloggers who only publish their work on Medium usually aren't going to be as successful as those bloggers who use both platforms.

When you use Medium, you will have the option of becoming a member. It costs five dollars a month to become a member, and it's worth spending your money.

Even if you only read articles on Medium, I would still recommend becoming a member. This is because the Medium membership allows you to read articles that aren't available to non-members.

Also, the money that you spend on your membership is given to Medium writers. It is much better for writers to receive money from you instead of advertisers.

When you are writing a draft version of your article, Medium makes it easy to make your article visually appealing. If you want to insert an image into your article, it is easy to do this with Medium.

It may take a little while to get used to all of Medium's features, but it's not complicated.

Another good way to learning Medium is to read articles about Medium its website. I suggest going to the Medium website and searching for Medium. By doing this, you will find what you need to know for getting the most out of the Medium website. Now, let's learn about images.

CHAPTER 12: IMAGES

Let's imagine that you are blogging on WordPress or Medium. You notice that a lot of the articles you see have images.

Not all the images you see in those articles are masterpieces, but you might be wondering how you could add images to your own articles. The good news is that adding images to articles isn't rocket science.

I will get you started with the basics in this chapter. The first step to adding images to articles is downloading some images to your laptop.

You don't need to be a photographer, or an artist, in order to get images for your blog. There are plenty of websites where you can find images which will help you attract readers.

My favorite website for images is Pixabay. At Pixabay, you will find over one million images you can use for your articles. You can use these images for free, and you will likely to find images that are relevant to your articles.

Since I'm not a lawyer, you will have to decide which images are legal for you to use with your articles. However, Pixabay is a reputable company with which I am comfortable using for great images.

After you have downloaded an image, you need to put that image into your article. Go to your WordPress website, using your Gutenberg editor to put an image into your article.

If you are putting an image at the top of your article, use the cover image block. Although, if you want to insert images into the rest of your article, you need to use the image block.

When you add images to your articles, Gutenberg will allow you to adjust the size of your images. The images then look good in your articles.

Medium also lets you add images to the articles which you write for their website. Once you get used to adding images to your online articles, you will wonder why you didn't do it before.

Usually I'm thinking of photographs when I think of images; however, images are much more than that. An online image can also be a chart, graph, still frame, infographic, or a comic.

The key to using images when you are blogging is to know what types of images are appropriate for your articles. If you are going to use images in your articles, use images that will attract readers. This is opposed to images that will turn them away.

While blogging, you have some advantages over traditional print articles of which you might not be aware. For instance, you can add color images to your online articles for free. However, if you were to use color images in a print article, it would be very expensive. So, don't be afraid to add color images to your online articles.

Now, let's look at another place where you can find the images you need for your articles. This is a website called Canva. It is a billion-dollar company located in Australia.

Recently, Canva bought Pixabay and a company called Pexels. As you learn more about Canva, you will want to spend more time on their website.

Canva has awesome graphic design software. It will not only help you find images for your articles, but you will be able to do many other things as well. For instance, they have templates that you can use to create a logo.

You might be wondering why you would need to have a logo? You should have a logo if you are serious about blogging, podcasting, and self-publishing.

When you have used Canva to design your logo, you can also use it to design business cards, brochures, and even the cover of your self-published book.

Although, unless you know what you are doing, I would recommend paying someone else to design your book cover. I'm still deciding whether or not to design the cover for this book.

The beauty of Canva is that, it not only allows you to find images, but it also helps you to create amazing marketing materials. If you haven't started using Canva yet, you need to start.

There are other top-notch websites where you can find images for your blog. I personally am a big fan of Unsplash. Unsplash's images are amazing. Here you will be able to find many free images for your articles.

Unsplash is a Canadian-based company. They have a good reputation for the photographs found on their website. Pixabay and Unsplash are the two main websites that I use when I need to find images for my blog.

I plan on using Pexels in the future. Canva now owns Pexels and Pixabay as I mentioned above.

If you use the websites that I have just shared, then you will have the image resources that you need for your blog. However, if you want to use a different strategy for finding images, that's alright too.

The main thing to understand is that you don't want to get sued for illegally using images. If you aren't sure whether or not you should use an image, don't use it.

The images that you use, are meant to enhance your articles. Don't risk your financial well-being with a rookie mistake. Instead, show some common sense whenever adding images to your articles.

We have covered a lot in this chapter. If you are serious about blogging, this is basic information that you need to know. Just remember that learning how to add images to your blog isn't as difficult as it seems.

CHAPTER 13: PROBLOGGER

I'm now going to teach you about ProBlogger, a website started by Darren Rowse. Rowse is an Australian man who shows people the right way to blog.

I have known about ProBlogger for quite a while, and I'm very impressed with how helpful Darren Rowse is. The ProBlogger website has both podcasts and articles.

Rowse is a genuine person who wants to help other people. The purpose of ProBlogger is to encourage people to start their own blogs. If you have already started a blog, then Darren Rowse will show you how to improve it.

Although I enjoy reading ProBlogger articles, I actually prefer listening to the ProBlogger podcasts. The advice Rowse gives you in these podcasts is based on his experience and expertise in blogging and podcasting.

Another thing Rowse teaches you is that it is possible to make money from your blog. Once you have a large number of enthusiastic people coming to your blog, it becomes very easy to monetize it.

While listening to the ProBlogger podcast, you will notice there is a consistent message. If you want to be a successful blogger, then you need to have a plan.

Many bloggers give up on blogging, because they haven't figured out what they are trying to accomplish. The reason I know so much about this is because I used to be a blogger who lacked focus.

I still don't have my blog planned out as well as I would like, but my WordPress blog is much better than it once was.

One thing I like, which Darren Rowse does well, is when he lets new bloggers tell their blogging stories on his podcast. This is great, because these new bloggers haven't yet made the big-time. Still, they are moving in the right direction.

You can definitely learn a lot by listening to the struggles and triumphs of beginning bloggers. I personally believe there is more to blogging than making money directly through a blog.

For those of you who are planning on writing a book, your blog can encourage your readers to buy your new book. You can further use your blog to convince your readers that they need to be included within your email list.

If you want to learn more about email marketing, I recommend reading the content marketing chapter of this book (chapter nine).

Even though I have said that I like the ProBlogger podcasts better than the articles, you should also read the articles. You will find great ideas in the articles which will help you with blogging.

Darren Rowse also has some other resources to help with your blogging. He has written several books about blogging, while also having a few blogging courses of which you can sign up.

I've neither read his books, nor signed up for his courses; although, a lot of bloggers have benefited from the content Rowse offers.

Many may not be aware that Darren Rowse is also interested in photography. Rowse has a website which helps you learn how to become a better photographer. You can find a link to this website on ProBlogger.

A nice feature of ProBlogger is that it makes you feel as if you are part of the blogging community. Darren Rowse doesn't just focus on himself, but rather he tries to celebrate the success of other bloggers.

As you are working on your blog, it's nice to know there are other bloggers, who are facing the same types of challenges with which you are struggling. One thing I will say about Darren Rowse is that he is a very hard worker. Not only does he do all the things that I have already mentioned, but he also holds ProBlogger conferences in Australia.

While it may not be practical for you to attend a blog conference in Australia, there is no reason you can't attend a similar conference in a location which is closer.

Other types of conferences, such as social media conferences, can be beneficial. If you think that attending conferences and conventions can inspire you to become a better blogger, then you should definitely attend some of them.

By attending these types of events, you are investing in your own education. Also, conferences and conventions are an awesome place for networking. I know that I will bring my business cards with me when I attend one of these events.

While you are on ProBlogger, you will quickly learn it is a good idea to diversify your income. For instance, don't become too reliant on page views for your blog.

If you rely too much on one source of income, you will be in a bad situation should that source of income decline. One possible idea for diversifying your income is to start a podcast.

I'm planning on starting a podcast as soon as possible. When I start my podcast, I plan on interviewing people once a week. Although podcasting is a bit different than blogging, they are both great methods of communicating.

As I mentioned earlier, sometimes Darren Rowse lets beginner bloggers tell their stories on his podcast. Usually these stories have already been recorded by the bloggers.

Then, Rowse explains at the beginning of each podcast what that episode will be about. After the bloggers share their stories, Rowse praises them while explaining the main takeaways to the listeners.

Even though ProBlogger is a great resource, it shouldn't be your only source. In the next chapter, I will show you how you can learn more about blogging through online video courses.

CHAPTER 14: UDEMY

You can learn many things by watching online video courses on Udemy. In this chapter, I will be focusing on how to use Udemy to improve your blogging skills. The first step is visiting the Udemy website.

Udemy offers both free and paid online courses. The courses I'm going to recommend are courses that cost a small amount of money. Usually, if you wait for the specials, then you can get most courses for ten dollars.

The first course for which I would suggest signing up is called: *Blogging for Beginners.* Salvador Briggman teaches this course, and he explains how he became a successful blogger.

In this course, Briggman has a lot of excellent advice for beginning bloggers. For instance, he suggests writing longer articles. Many new bloggers might be comfortable with this.

Through his course, Salvador Briggman convinced me that I should start writing longer articles. It takes me a lot longer to write a two-thousand-word article, but I know that it's worth the effort.

More importantly, through the *Blogging for Beginners* course I learned that I needed to switch from WordPress.com to WordPress.org.

Actually, I already knew that I should switch to WordPress.org, but Briggman was the first person who persuaded me to do it.

Now, I'm going to recommend another blogging course that Udemy offers. This course is called: *Blogging Masterclass*. It is taught by Brad Merrill. Merrill is someone who knows what he's talking about.

In this course, you will learn about blogging from someone who has already been successful as a popular technology blogger. Brad Merrill believes that a blogger needs to show discipline with their blogging.

If you are someone who needs to be inspired before you can write, Merrill doesn't have much sympathy for you. However, many successful writers would agree with him on this point.

As I have previously mentioned , I force myself to write a little bit each day. I would end up writing about two or three days per year if I waited to be inspired.

Of course, I am going to spend more time working on my book than I do working on my blogs. However, I still am very serious about my WordPress and Medium blogs.

Speaking of Medium, I recommend signing up for the Medium Blogging Masterclass. I briefly mentioned this course in *Medium* (chapter eleven).

In this course taught by Sinem Gunel, you will learn how to get your articles published on Medium. Gunel will also give you good ideas on how to write your articles.

There is a lot more to blogging on Medium than you might think. So, let Sinem Gunel guide you. Through the *Medium Blogging Masterclass,* you will also learn how to use Trello - an online productivity tool.

In this course, Gunel let's Philip Hofmacher teach the Trello part of her *Medium Blogging Masterclass.* Hofmacher is Gunel's boyfriend, and he is very enthusiastic about Trello.

I also like Trello, but I primarily use Trello as my online to-do list. If you want to understand how to use Trello, I suggest listening to what Philip Hofmacher has to say. Hofmacher has a strong accent, so you will have to listen very carefully.

Part of being a good blogger is knowing how to build your own website. This skill that can be learned. Before long, you will be able to create a WordPress website of which you can be proud.

A perfect course for this is called: *Wordpress for Beginners.* Andrew Williams teaches this course, as well as many other Udemy courses.

Williams teaches you the difference between posts and pages. He also teaches you about tags, legal pages, and how to create navigation for your website.

In addition to the *WordPress for Beginners* course, it will show you how to protect your website with security features. Andrew Williams is a knowledgeable instructor, guiding you step-by-step in your WordPress journey.

You will find valuable information in unexpected places while you are learning about blogging. For example, you might be searching for blogging courses on Udemy, and not find the type of course in which you are interested.

If this happens, the best thing to do is to search for courses that are related to blogging. I suggest searching for content marketing courses.

Content marketing courses will not only teach you how to market your online articles, but will also show you how to market your book.

I recommend signing up for the *Content is King* course. This Udemy course is taught by Steve McDonald. The course will teach you how to write better content.

Steve McDonald will also teach how to market your content. Earlier in this book, I wrote an entire chapter about content marketing. If you haven't read that chapter yet, go ahead and do so now.

In the *Content is King* course, you will learn the difference between evergreen and trending content. McDonald will also teach you how to understand your audience, as well as the importance of using keywords.

Steve McDonald offers the *Content is King* course as a book. If you take the *Content is King* course, you will be glad that you did.

We have discussed how to use Udemy, as a resource, helps you with your blogging. Believe it or not, I have only scratched the surface of the video courses that are available on Udemy.

The main takeaway from this chapter is that there are plenty of online resources available. These will assist you if you want to learn how to blog.

SECTION III: SELF-PUBLISHING

CHAPTER 15: NO MORE GATEKEEPERS

Now we are ready to begin the third section of this book. This is my favorite section, and this is my favorite chapter. So, let's get started.

When I told people I was writing this book, most of them asked how I was going to publish it. For some reason, they seemed to think that publishing a book was a difficult task.

In the old days, it was difficult to self-publish a book. However, that was then and this is now. The publishing gatekeepers of the past no longer wield the power that they once did.

There have been changes in technology over the past few decades which have disrupted the publishing industry. If you want to self-publish your own book now, you don't have to ask for anyone's permission. You just do it.

However, you still need to approach your writing in a professional manner if want to be a successful self-publisher,. Also, as a self-publisher, you need to first learn a little bit about marketing.

Fortunately, there are many excellent resources to help you learn the details of book marketing. I believe the best online resource for learning how to market you book is *The Creative Penn* podcast.

This podcast was started by Joanna Penn, and features interviews with talented writers who have had success with self-publishing. The interviews in the podcast episodes are lengthy, but it is well worth your time to listen to them.

I will provide more information about *The Creative Penn* podcast in *The Creative Penn* - chapter seventeen of this book.

Moreover, when you are self-publishing, keep in mind the amount of money you are spending. On the one hand, you don't want to be extravagant. You also don't want to be so cheap that you end up self-publishing a book of which you aren't proud.

You will need to decide what type of book you want to create. For instance, you can self-publish your book as a paperback, hardcover, eBook or audio book.

I plan on publishing this book as a paperback, eBook and audio book. You can also publish your book in foreign languages if that interests you.

Some people like to use the term indie-publishing instead of self-publishing. I did some research on this, and came to the conclusion that nearly everyone has a different opinion on what these two terms mean.

If you want to argue with people at cocktail parties, then I suppose you should know the difference between indie-publishing and self-publishing. For the purposes of this book, however, both of these terms mean the same thing.

As I have mentioned previously, the publishing gatekeepers aren't as powerful as they once were. This is a good thing. Now you don't have to beg someone to publish your book.

Also, you don't have to publish your book on the traditional publisher's schedule. If you wait for the traditional publisher's approval, much of the information in your book will be outdated before anyone has a chance to read it.

When you are a self-publisher, your purpose is to share your ideas with the public. Although writing a book isn't easy, it is very rewarding. Writing allows you to express your creativity in a way that isn't always possible.

Don't let the gatekeepers rob you of this.

Even if you never make a penny directly through your writing, I still recommend self-publishing your non-fiction and fiction books. Your writing will establish you as an expert.

You might not think of yourself as an expert, but after you write a book, others will. There is no need to feel awkward about being an expert. Just realize that, through your writing, you have touched other people's lives.

We will discuss becoming an expert in more detail within the next chapter.

When you have finished writing your book, you must decide how to distribute your book. Amazon is the biggest when it comes to distributing your book to your readers.

However, you can use more than one distributor for your book: Kobo, Apple Books, and Barnes & Noble.

To make things even more complicated, there are also aggregators. An aggregator is a service that automatically gets your book distributed through several different distributors. You need to realize that, even if you are working with book distributors or book aggregators, that you are still the one who is responsible for marketing your book. Distributors and aggregators can help you, but they can't do everything.

Even if you don't have marketing experience, you will still have to be the main person who markets your book. Fortunately, there are plenty of excellent online resources which will teach you how to successfully sell your book.

As I mentioned previously, *The Creative Penn* podcast is the best online resource for learning how to market your book.

Another marketing resource that I recommend, is *14 Steps to Self-Publishing a Book.* You can read the eBook version of this book. It was written by Mike Kowis, and is available on Kindle Unlimited for free.

Hopefully you have already signed up with this service, so that you can begin reading this book immediately. In this book, Kowis explains how to self-publish a book.

It took Mike Kowis a while to figure out how self-publish his books. Now, though, he is willing to share his knowledge with you.

The main takeaway from this chapter is this: it is no longer necessary to grovel and beg in order to get your book published. If you are a former American president, or a First Lady, then go ahead and use a traditional publisher for your book.

However, for the rest of us, self- publishing makes the most sense. So, now is the best time to start writing your absolutely amazing book.

CHAPTER 16: BECOMING AN EXPERT

One of the great benefits of writing a book is that, after your book is published, you will be considered an expert. You may have been an expert before you wrote your book, but after your book is written, people will start taking you more seriously.

The reason people will respect you is because most people have never written a book. It certainly isn't easy to write a book. If it was easy, everybody would be doing it.

Sometimes it is difficult to convert your thoughts into words while writing your book. There are also times when your ideas might make sense to you, but they might not make sense to your readers. Therefore, carefully consider your choice of words.

I don't mention this to discourage you from writing a book. The point I'm making is that the struggle to write coherent sentences also helps you grow.

Even if you only write a short book, you will learn a lot about the topic and about yourself. I believe this concept is true whether you are writing non-fiction or a novella.

It is my educated guess that, when I write my novella, I will become an even better writer than I currently am. So, when you write your book and you self-publish it, you will have already established yourself as an expert in several topics. First of all, you will be an expert in writing; and secondly, you will be an expert in self-publishing.

You may think that I'm using the term expert too loosely. However, I don't believe that I am. Just think of an expert as someone who has specialized knowledge. They are willing to share this knowledge with others.

Sometimes, as an expert, it will make sense to share your knowledge without expecting to be paid. You don't need to be paid for every single thought that's floating around inside of your head.

That being said, there is nothing wrong with being paid for sharing your expertise. Your time is valuable, and you happen to have many of the answers for which other people are looking.

For example, some authors not only write books, but they also help other struggling writers who need a bit of advice. Believe it or not, some writers make a substantial portion of their income by teaching beginning writers the basics of book writing.

This type of service is called being a writing coach or a book coach. It is similar to taking a writing class, but it is far more specialized.

A writing coach will help her clients organize their ideas, making sure that they get some words written down each day.

Writing coaches also show their clients how to self-publish their books.

After I finish writing this book, I plan on becoming a writing coach. This doesn't mean I won't continue to write my own books. It just means that I want to get into the trenches, while helping other writers who are struggling to write their own books.

For some writers, reading this book will be enough coaching to help them finish writing their book. Although, some writers may need my individual coaching. If I believe that I can help them, I will.

Let's get back to discussing how writing and self-publishing your book can help you become an expert. As I have previously said, you will become an expert in writing and self-publishing when you write and self-publish your book.

Having said this, you are going to need a cover for your self-published book. Even if you only publish your book as an eBook, you will still need some sort of book cover.

You could pay someone to design your book cover, but what if you designed your own book cover? I'm not telling you that you should design your own book cover; but, if you did, then you would also become an expert in book cover design.

Are you beginning to see how easy it is to become an expert? Part of being an expert is simply having the self-confidence to acknowledge that you are one.

I'm not talking about having an over-inflated ego. Don't be like the person who enters a singing contest when they can't even carry a tune.

Many people are too modest. If you are one of these people, than I hereby give you permission to toot your own horn. As long as you don't get carried away with it, it's alright to feel good about yourself.

Let me give you an example of someone who improved himself through writing a book. When Victor Hugo wrote *The Hunchback of Notre-Dame,* he was already an expert in French history.

However, by writing this book, he took his level of expertise to a whole new level. Not only did Hugo expand his knowledge of French history, but he also became an expert in French architecture through writing this book.

Now that the Cathedral of Notre-Dame has been severely damaged by a fire, *The Hunchback of Notre-Dame* becomes an even more significant novel. If you are searching for a writer from which to learn, spend your time studying Victor Hugo.

I hope you are beginning to realize you don't have to be a genius before you can become an expert. Becoming an expert is a gradual process, but it can be achieved in a timely manner under the right circumstances.

This is the beauty of writing a book. When you write your book, you will learn your topic in more detail. Then, you understand it more than you previously thought was possible. Your book will show others that you truly are an expert.

So, becoming an expert is certainly a great reason for writing and self-publishing a book. Seize the day and begin writing your book immediately.

CHAPTER 17: THE CREATIVE PENN

The Creative Penn is a website which Joanna Penn created. I am very impressed with this website. The part of this website with which I'm most impressed is the podcast.

Therefore, this chapter will primarily be focused on *The Creative Penn* podcast. In her podcast, Joanna Penn interviews writers, as well as people who have experience in self-publishing.

The great thing about her podcast is that it will teach you how to distribute and market your book. When self-publishing your book, you are going to need to learn how to market it.

This is why you need to start listening to *The Creative Penn* podcast. The interviews in this podcast are brilliant. They will teach you exactly what you need to know.

Joanna Penn conducts the interviews, and in the process, she has some informative conversations with many successful authors. However, before the interviews, Penn talks a little bit about some of her own ideas.

Most of Penn's podcast episodes last about an hour. You will thereby need to set aside some time if you want to listen to an entire episode in one sitting.

Sometimes I will reward myself by listening to a podcast episode after I have made some progress on this book. Since I keep myself very busy, I'm not able to listen to *The Creative Penn* every day.

I always enjoy listening to *The Creative Penn*; although, I will admit some episodes are better than others. In this chapter, I will be encouraging you to listen to this podcast.

Don't just listen to the interviews, but also take action. It is easy to listen to good advice and then do absolutely nothing. You must make writing a priority when you are writing your book.

This doesn't mean that there aren't other important things going on in your life. Certainly, no sensible person would ever tell you to neglect your family or friends.

However, getting your book written is also important. While writing can be time consuming, it doesn't have to take up your entire day. On days when you are especially busy, you will need to make sure that you still get some words written down.

As I have previously stated in this book, I work a full-time job. Still, I found the time I needed to write this book. So, if writing a book is one of your top priorities, you will have plenty of time to write it.

Now, let's explore *The Creative Penn* podcast. The first episode in which I recommend listening is episode #309 - an interview with Chris Brogan. I have known about Chris Brogan for many years, so it was great to listen to this podcast.

Brogan is someone who has self-published some of his books. He has used traditional publishers when he thought it was appropriate.

Chris Brogan is a bit of a loose cannon, so it is always interesting to hear what he has to say. In this particular interview, Brogan not only talks about his successful books and his least successful book.

The book that was Brogan's biggest commercial flop was titled: *The Freaks Shall Inherit the Earth.* For what it's worth, I thought this was his best book; although, I haven't read all of his books.

The Freaks book shows how oddballs are often capable of accomplishing great things. This book is a perfect example of how a book can have literary merit. Still, it may not be commercially successful.

Now let's find another noteworthy interview on *The Creative Penn.* The next podcast episode that I would recommend is episode #394. This episode is an interview with Amber Rae.

I had never heard of Rae before, but she has very good advice for beginning authors. Amber Rae realizes that many beginning authors worry too much. This is bad, because if you are paralyzed with fear, then you are never going to be a very good writer.

This podcast episode is especially entertaining. Rae uses a lot of funny voices to describe different emotions that she was feeling when she was writing her book.

While I haven't yet read Amber Rae's book, it is obvious from this interview that she has many important ideas. Rae's central message in this podcast episode is that writers should choose the emotion of wonder.

Amber Rae also teaches us that worry is alright under certain circumstances. However, generally speaking, book authors worry too much.

Joanna Penn has conducted so many excellent interviews. I'm not always completely sure which episodes I should highlight. Nevertheless, I promise that I will not allow my writing to be slowed down by worry.

The next podcast episode that I suggest is episode #330. This episode is an interview with Jeff Goins. In this interview, he promotes his book: *Real Artists Don't Starve.* I haven't read this book yet, but it sounds like it is a valuable resource.

Goins also recommends making money from several different things, instead of relying only on book sales. He has used this approach with his own business, and it has worked out quite well for him.

One other thing you will learn from Jeff Goins is that he admires Charles Handy. Handy is an economist who has interesting ideas on several different topics. I had to do a DuckDuckGo search, in order to figure out exactly who Charles Handy is.

As you can see, listening to *The Creative Penn* podcast is a wise use of your time. I also recommend exploring some of the other resources on *The Creative Penn* website.

Joanna Penn can certainly teach you a lot if you are a teachable person. I know that I have already learned quite a bit from her, as well as the people that she interviews. So, take the time to listen to *The Creative Penn* podcast.

CHAPTER 18: PRINT-ON-DEMAND

Print-on-Demand is an amazing technology which we will discuss in this chapter. When you use print-on-demand, you can just print the books your customers have ordered, instead of storing thousands of books in your garage.

Print-on-demand lets you print hardback or paperback books. What's nice is that you don't have to own any special machinery to get started with the print-on-demand technology.

Sometimes print-on-demand is abbreviated as POD. It doesn't really matter whether you spell the entire term, or if you abbreviate it. What actually matters is that you fully understand what this technology can do for you.

First of all, it's important to realize you will probably make more money with your eBooks than you will with hardbacks or paperbacks. That being said, there is nothing that can replace holding a book in your hand.

Some younger people might not understand this sentiment, but if you are an old-timer like me, you sure do. I'm not planning on publishing this book as a hardback, but I will be publishing it as a paperback.

Still, if you want to publish your book as a hardback, go for it. Some of your customers may actually prefer to read your book in a hardback format.

Even if you are not interested in publishing a print-on-demand book, I would still recommend doing it.

The reasons I will give you for publishing a print-on-demand book have nothing to do with nostalgia. Indeed, the reasons that I will give you are based on common sense.

First of all, most book authors don't make all their money from the books that they write. If you are one of those lucky authors who makes the vast majority of your money through writing, then that's awesome.

Many authors, though, rely on coaching, consulting, public speaking, and selling products for part of their income. This is where your print-on-demand paperback book comes in handy.

Let's say, for instance, that you are attending a public event. You tell some of the people that you are a published author. Now, let's further suppose that some of these people would like to learn how to write their own book.

Can you imagine what a thrill it would be if you handed them a free copy of your book on that topic? The only thing which would be better is if you also autographed it for them.

If you are a writing coach, this would be a great way to find new clients. You might be wondering: If people read my book, then why would they need my coaching? Well, some people won't need your coaching.

However, there will be many people who would be willing to pay you, for your expertise. As good as your book may be, there are some beginning writers who will also want your coaching.

I know there were times, when I could have used a book writing coach while I was writing this book.

The main point I'm trying to make is that you can use your paperback book like a business card. Obviously, though, you don't want to hand out so many free books that you end up in the poorhouse.

There is nothing wrong with handing out a few autographed books from time to time. Just remember that you will have to be the one who decides when this marketing tactic is appropriate.

Paperback books are also good for book signings. Although my mother isn't a published author, she is continually reminding me that I need to have some book signings.

If all you have are eBooks and audio books, then it's going to be pretty hard to have book signings. You will be able to meet your potential fans in person.

Book signings, too, allow you to go on a book tour. Since you will be a self-published author, you can create a book tour that is convenient for you.

On my book tour, I will be focusing on book signings that are within fifty miles of my home. I don't have the details of my book tour figured out yet, and that is okay. My biggest goal right now is to finish writing the last few chapters of this book.

While you are self-publishing your paperback book, you will have several different companies that can help you. One company that many authors like to use for print-on-demand is Amazon.

Since Amazon is in the business of selling books, you should consider self-publishing your book through Kindle Direct Publishing. Kindle Direct Publishing is also known as KDP.

Until recently, authors would self-publish their Amazon paperback books through a service called CreateSpace. However, now Amazon has moved everything from CreateSpace over to KDP.

If you use KDP, or any other print-on-demand service, you will need to buy an ISBN number. Don't get your ISBN number through KDP or any other print-on-demand service.

Instead, buy your ISBN number directly from Bowker if you live in the United States. If you live in England, then you should buy you ISBN number through Nielsen.

For other countries, you will have to research where you should buy your ISBN number. I can't emphasize enough that you need to get this part of the self-publishing process right. I know this may seem like a tedious detail, but this is something that needs to be done.

Another step to self-publishing your paperback book is making sure you get your book copyrighted. I know that you don't want to spend your time thinking about copyright law, but this is something about which you must learn.

We have covered a lot of ground in this chapter. I hope that you are excited about the opportunities that print-on-demand technology has created for writers.

CHAPTER 19: EBOOKS

eBooks are a great option if you want to make money directly from your books. I have to admit that, before I signed up for Kindle Unlimited, my experience with eBooks was minimal.

Many readers are already accustomed to reading eBooks, so you will probably sell far more eBooks than paperbacks. Usually, though, most authors charge less money for their eBooks than they do for their paperbacks.

My suggestion is to sell your book as an eBook, paperback, and/or audio book. Your job as an author is to let the public read your book however they prefer. When I'm reading eBooks, I enjoy reading them on my laptop.

While some people like to read their eBooks on smaller devices, I prefer reading my eBooks on a larger screen. Though, you need to self-publish your book in whatever format is appealing to your readers.

One nice thing about self-publishing an eBook is that it is easier than self-publishing a print-on-demand book. When you are self-publishing your eBook, I would recommend getting an ISBN number for it.

People will tell you don't need an ISBN number for your eBook, but they are wrong. For every reason why you shouldn't get an ISBN number for your eBook, there are a dozen reasons why you should.

Since you are probably already planning on self-publishing a paperback book with an ISBN number, take a little extra effort. Put an ISBN number on your eBook as well.

When you buy you ISBN number for your paperback from Bowker, you have the option of buying more than one ISBN number. I recommend buying a pack of ten ISBN numbers. It's expensive, but it's worth it.

You are probably wondering: What will I do with ten ISBN numbers? Well, once you self-publish your first book, it is very likely you will want to write more books. So, plan ahead and buy a pack of ten ISBN numbers from Bowker.

As stated in the previous chapter, if you don't live in the United States, then your ISBN numbers will have to be bought through a different company.

However, the great thing about ISBN numbers is that they never expire. Just think of the purchasing ISBN numbers as an investment in your writing career.

You are also going to need an ISBN number for your audio book. The more ways you self-publish your book, the more ISBN numbers that you will use. Though, this is alright; part of being a professional writer is learning how to properly handle the business side of your profession.

When you are self-publishing your eBook and your paperback book, it can be confusing. It's a steep learning curve, but with a little patience, you can learn how to self-publish your book.

If you don't consider yourself patient, then now is the best time to cultivate this important character trait. Patience is a virtue when it comes to self-publishing.

There are many companies you can use to distribute your book, but two companies I suggest are: Kindle Direct Publishing and IngramSpark.

Amazon will try to persuade you to exclusively self-publish your eBook through KDP. However, I think it is better to also distribute your book through IngramSpark. You may not have heard of IngramSpark, but they are a big player of which you need to be aware.

You are leaving a lot of money on the table if you only self-publish your book with Kindle Direct Publishing. Your job as an author is to give as many people as possible the opportunity to buy your book.

If you want to self-publish a hardback version of your book, then you will need IngramSpark for this. After all, KDP doesn't offer this service.

IngramSpark will also distribute your eBook to places that KDP won't. For instance, IngramSpark will distribute your eBook to Kobo, Apple, and Barnes & Noble.

This is why it's sensible to self-publish through both IngramSpark and KDP. Both of these companies can help you accomplish your goal of making your book available to the public.

In order to be a successful author, you sometimes have to wear your entrepreneur's hat. You don't need to be an especially clever entrepreneur, but you do need to know a little bit about how to market your book.

The more that you learn about self-publishing, the more excited you will become about the opportunities which exist for authors. For example, I will teach you some things about audio books (of which you may not be aware) in the next chapter.

As I have been writing this book, I keep discovering new ways that I will be able to make money. Right now, my writing is just a side hustle. Although, I believe that it will become much more than that.

The nice thing about self-publishing and blogging is that you have the potential of creating your own business. While you might not think of yourself as an entrepreneur, that is exactly what you will be.

If you are not comfortable with public speaking, I recommend signing up with a Toastmaster's Club. I was the president of my Toastmaster's Club many years ago and I loved it.

It may sound strange that you need to learn how to speak. After all, you really just want to write. Learning how to speak in public, however, will prepare you for your book signings.

I know that I have covered some things in this chapter that aren't directly related to eBooks. This is because I want to fully prepare you for opportunities available to you once you are a self-published author.

Now, let's learn about audio books.

CHAPTER 20: AUDIO BOOKS

When most people think about self-publishing, they are probably thinking about paperback books and eBooks. Conversely, I suggest that you also self-publish an audio book.

Self-publishing an audio book may sound like an expensive endeavor, but it doesn't need to be. One of the first decisions that you will need to make is: Who will narrate your audio book?

You can narrate your audio book, or you can pay someone else to do it. If you are going to narrate your own book, then you will need to learn how to do so in a professional manner.

There are online courses on Udemy that can teach you this. The best course that I have seen is called: *How to Master Audible Work from Home*. This brilliant online course is taught by Bailey Varness.

This course is designed for people who want to make their living narrating books. Since Varness has already narrated sixty-five books, she certainly knows what she is talking about.

When Bailey Varness reveals she is a terrible typist, I actually found that to be an endearing quality. Watching this course will help you make up your mind whether or not you want to narrate your own audio book.

If you decide to pay someone else to narrate your book, you have a couple of different options. The first option is to pay someone by the hour. Some hourly rates which narrators charge may seem expensive.

Although, when you realize that professional narrators spend a lot of time editing their audio recordings, you realize that they are only being paid a fair price for their work.

Another way to pay your narrator is to give her a percentage of the royalties from your audio book. If your audio book doesn't sell many copies, though, your narrator isn't going to make much money.

The last method of payment for narrators is called a stipend. To be honest, I don't fully understand what a stipend is. However, there seems to be a formula that determines whether your audio book narrator is eligible to receive a stipend.

When you are ready to create your audio book, you will need to decide which company should distribute it. The biggest audio book distributor is ACX. Amazon owns ACX, because why wouldn't they?

I still haven't decided which book distributor I plan on using for my audio book. So, instead of talking about ACX, I will mention a few of the alternatives to ACX.

Findaway Voices is an audio book distributor with which many people are happy. If you distribute your audio book through their company, then you will be able to keep a large percentage of your royalties.

Also, Findaway Voices will help you find a narrator for your audio book. One big advantage Findaway Voices has over ACX is that they will let you decide on the price you want to set for your audio book.

Even though I am against authors overcharging for their audio books, I also don't think this is a decision ACX should be making. So, needless to say, I'm very impressed with Findaway Voices.

Now let's consider another audio book distributor called: ListenUp. ListenUp is located in Atlanta, and their philosophy about audio books is similar to what Findaway Voices believes.

The more research I do on audio books, the more I realize how important it is to understand the business side of self-publishing. Even if you don't think of yourself as a savvy entrepreneur, you still need to have a basic strategy for making money from the books you write. If you aren't careful, you will end up making bad business decisions which you will regret.

Spending most of your free time writing doesn't mean that you should neglect learning the business basics of self-publishing.

So let's look at one more possible audio book distributor before we move onto other things in this chapter. The final distributor I will mention to you is called: Author's Republic.

With Author's Republic, you have an additional option for your audio book's distribution. However, Author's Republic doesn't directly help you create your audio book. Instead, they specialize in distributing your audio book.

If you don't mind working with a different company for creating your audio book, then Author's Republic might be the audio book distributor for which you are looking.

Obviously, my commentary about audio book distributors in this chapter hasn't been comprehensive. However, I feel that I have shared enough information with you to get you started on your audio book creation journey.

Now that we know a little bit about audio book distributors, it is time that we also learned more about audio book retailers. Indeed, when most readers think about audio books, they primarily are thinking about companies such as Audible and Barnes & Noble.

Of course Audible is owned by Amazon. In case you haven't noticed it yet, Amazon is a very large company that owns nearly everything which is worth owning.

To be honest, most readers only want to know where they can find a good audio book. The companies that provide access to audio books are called audio book retailers. These retailers receive their audio books from audio book distributors. This is why you need to do some research on the audio book distributor with which you choose to work.

Before I conclude this chapter, I want to recommend using Google Audiobooks for listening to your favorite books. This is the audio book retailer that I use, and I really enjoy listening to audio books on their website.

The main takeaway from this chapter is that you need to self-publish your book as an audio book. Now, let's move on to the final chapter.

CHAPTER 21: GOODREADS

I can sometimes be critical of Amazon; although, I have nothing but good things to say about Goodreads. Several years ago, Amazon bought Goodreads. I recommend that you spend some time learning how to use this website.

Even if you don't plan on becoming an author, Goodreads is a great place to hang out. If you love books, you will be very comfortable using Goodreads.

Goodreads lets you discuss the books that you have read, while also sharing the books that you are currently reading. Even though I haven't used the Goodreads website as much as I ought to, I plan on doing better very soon.

If you plan on becoming an author, then it is more important you start spending some of your time on Goodreads. There are millions of readers and authors who use this website. And, they would enjoy learning about the book that you are writing.

The purpose of Goodreads isn't to spend all of your time talking about yourself. However, after you have self-published your book, many readers on this website will genuinely want to learn more about you and your book.

When you become an author, you will have accomplished something which most other people haven't. Instead of being someone who is planning on writing a book, you will be someone who has actually written a book.

After you seriously start looking at the Goodreads website, you will quickly realize why so many readers and authors spend so much time there.

For instance, I just finished reading an eBook, so I reviewed it on Goodreads. My review of this eBook was only two sentences long, but at least it's a start.

After I left my book review, I noticed that some other people had also reviewed this eBook. I guess that I should reveal that this 88-page eBook was about podcasting.

Some of the reviewers really hated this eBook, but other reviewers thought that it was great. While I didn't write much in my review, I thought that this podcasting eBook was good. And so, I gave it four out of five stars.

I personally think that, if any book that can keep my interest long enough for me to finish it, then has to have some merit. However, if you are going to be an author, sometimes you need to have thick skin.

Another feature Goodreads has are groups. So far, I have signed up for one group, and I will probably join a few more. To be honest, I'm surprised how many groups there are on Goodreads.

Although I have known about Goodreads for many years, it wasn't until recently that I started actually learning how to use it. In the past, I would look at the website and that's about as far as it went.

Yet, things changed for me when I enrolled in an online course on Udemy which explained how to use Goodreads. This course is called: *Goodreads For Authors.* It was taught by Cathy Presland and Michelle Booth.

As I started watching the videos in this course, I quickly realized that there are benefits to using Goodreads of which I had never suspected. For example, not only can you join groups on this website, but you can also make friends with people.

Some people familiar with Goodreads may think they already know how to use this website. I am guessing, though, that most people still have a lot to learn when it comes to getting the most out of Goodreads.

The nice thing about learning is that, the more you learn, the more that you want to learn. So, of course, I signed up for another Udemy course about Goodreads.

This time, the course was called: *The Author's Guide to Goodreads,* taught by Barb Drozdowich. This is also an excellent course that can teach you what you need to know.

The first thing will need to know is how to sign up to be a member of Goodreads. If you are already a member, that's even better. Signing up for Goodreads is similar to becoming a member of Facebook or Twitter.

After you have joined Goodreads, you can begin learning how to navigate the website. Since Goodreads has a lot of features, it will take a while to figure everything out.

You don't have to learn every detail about Goodreads; although, it is good to learn as much as you can about this unique website. Your main focus while using Goodreads should be to network with other readers and writers.

One nice thing about Goodreads is that it helps you to find books in which you might be interested in reading. On Goodreads, not all of the big shots on the website will want to become your close, personal friends.

However, there is nothing to prevent you from following famous authors. Indeed, after you have written your first book, there may be people who will be interested in following you.

It is up to you how much information that you are willing to share with other people. Your privacy is something that should be protected, but if you are too frightened of the outside world, then you are going to miss out on a lot of important opportunities.

If you are interested in reading, and writing, then you should start using Goodreads immediately. Also, if you have friends on Facebook or Twitter who use Goodreads, you can connect with them on the Goodreads website.

After you have written your first book, you will realize that you will need some book reviews. These will help you sell more copies of your book. So, ask some of your friends on Goodreads if they would be willing to write a review for your amazing book.

CONCLUSION

If you have read this entire book, then you have all the information that you need to begin blogging and write your first book. When I started writing this book, I worried that I wouldn't have the persistence that is necessary to actually complete a book.

So let my example be an encouragement to you. You can write a book, even if you are not sure of yourself. In the past, I tried many times to write a book and failed.

Nevertheless, now that I have figured out how to write a book, I want to help other people with their writing. Just remember, that if you want to write your first book, then I have nothing but admiration for you.

THE END

ACKNOWLEDGEMENTS

Now is the time to thank those people who showed an interest in this book, even before I finished writing it. Here is a list of those people: Marcie Morgan; Mariela Harris; Samantha Ballard; David Ballard; Jackie Smith; Keith Smith; Miriam Watkins; Marcia Meade; Nathan Nelson; Tahy Alvin; Carla Hill; and Jason Alexander.

WRITING, BLOGGING, AND SELF-PUBLISHING

Have you ever thought about writing a book? Maybe you have tried more then once and failed. This is why you need to learn the secret writing formula which Kris Ballard has created.

Ballard tried for many years to write a book, and began to wonder whether he would ever succeed. This book that you are looking at, is proof that he found a way to accomplish his goal.

Writing a book isn't easy. If it was, everybody would be doing it. So let Ballard eliminate the stumbling blocks that are preventing the completion of your book.

As an added bonus, Ballard will also teach you how to write online articles. In order to do this, you will need create your own website. Fortunately the author has experience with this, so he can guide you.

Now is the best time to write your first book. The sense of accomplishment that you will feel, when you finish your rough draft is amazing.

So what are you waiting for? Read this book now, and then start writing your own book.

Made in the USA
Monee, IL
04 November 2026

67384417R00079